10 PROVEN WAYS TO RELIEVE STRESS NOW
An essential hack for a better life

VINH NGUYEN

CONTENTS

INTRODUCTION

Stress is not always bad! But avoidable stress is forever bad!

Do not get confused. I will explain. Everyone hates the feeling of fatigue (and frustration) that comes with being stressed. We do not like being stretched beyond our usual limits, and it shows in the way we react to stressful situations. That is why most people hate even the thought of being stressed. When we are stressed, we may underperform at our tasks and find little happiness in the things we do. That is why we all try to avoid stress.

However, stress itself is not bad. It is a defense mechanism that our body engages in to deal with difficult circumstances. It allows us to perform at levels higher than our usual limits to solve pressing issues. Stress can help you stay up for longer than usual to complete a task or give you extra endurance to escape from life-threatening danger. Stress gives us the extra capacity to perform intensely for a short period. Stress allows us to function in a high-performance mode to deal with complex or challenging situations. However, when stress becomes a permanent fixture in your life (or routine), there is a big problem.

It's like having an alarm clock permanently switched on without a snooze option. In the end, it will cause irreparable damage to you. That is why stress must not be allowed to become chronic and a part of your routine. That is why you must always look for ways to relieve yourself of the stress you face. That is why you must forever search for solutions to the stressors around you. And that is why I have written this book for you.

Are you forever stressed out and in need of relief? Do you want to know how to be more productive and enjoy your work? Do you want to learn new hacks for staying fresher for longer? If you have answered "Yes" to any of these questions, then this book is for you.

I know how dangerous stress can be—I have seen its firsthand effects. I know how it can destroy one's health and make one a shell of their usual self. I know how stress can catalyze the onset of conditions like anxiety and depression. But fortunately, I also know how to deal with the most common stressors around us, and my goal is to show you great techniques that can help you, too.

Stress gradually builds up within our lives when we do not take effective control of our time and what we spend it on. Unchallenged, chronic stress can grow to become the biggest threat to one's happiness and productivity. That is why you need to throw it out of your life boldly, starting from this moment. In the next few chapters, I will be showing you the techniques I used to deal with chronic stress and how you can adapt them for maximal efficiency.

Good luck!

CHAPTER 1

DEMYSTIFYING STRESS

"It's not stress that kills us; it is our reaction to it."
—Hans Selye

Considering how hard we try to avoid it, it is ironic that we need stress a lot. Yes, we need stress!

Without stress, we would drift through life without direction, motivation, and any inkling of how it feels to be excited about anything. Stress provides that burst of energy that stimulates our nervous system. When you feel physical or emotional tension (which is what we call stress), your body modifies itself to rise to the challenge. The body enters the fight-or-flight mode in reaction to this warning. The brain then releases vital chemicals (such as adrenaline and cortisol) into the bloodstream to facilitate this response. The heart rate increases, and the body diverts blood flow from vital organs into the extremities. This makes you more alert, focused, faster, stronger, and even smarter than usual.

This is how external and internal factors jolt us into taking action, whether to run from a predator or go for what we want. So there you have it. Stress is responsible for our inspiration and motivation. Its effects quicken our pulses and generate our emotions, which we call excitement and anticipation, or in a large dose, fear and apprehension.

Stress is a psychological response that allows us to temporarily expand our physical, cognitive, and mental abilities to react to a threat. That threat could be an impending deadline, an oncoming car, or a bad relationship. Stress leads us to the flight-or-fight response that grants us the endurance to either flee from the threat or deal with it decisively. It is stress that allows you to stay awake till the early hours of the day to ace an examination. It is stress that allows you to smash your work records to meet a deadline.

But the keyword in the definition of stress should be "temporarily." Stress puts us in a high-performance mode, but our body is not built to be in this mode permanently. When stress becomes a consistent companion, it causes wear and tear. You begin to forget to turn off that high-performance mode, and that will put you in a lot of trouble.

Acute stress versus chronic stress

Acute stress is the most common type of stress—it refers to threats that require an immediate response from you. That is the kind of stress you get when you cannot find your keys or get stuck in traffic. The distress can cause you to react wildly or suffer emotional dips. It may be bad, or it may be good; it may get us excited or afraid.

Stress becomes chronic when the same acute stressor triggers you so consistently and repeatedly that it becomes a long-term companion. When you continue to start your day by getting stuck in traffic or procrastination causes you to chase deadlines at work every day, it becomes chronic stress. It occurs when stress builds up in the body without relief over an extended period. When we are exposed to constant stressors, even the good kind, the body starts to suffer because it cannot return to its resting state. It remains in a condition/state that it cannot handle and was only meant to be in for a short period.

Acute or chronic, excessive (unmanaged) stress is dangerous. Let me cite an example here. In soccer, a penalty kick can be extremely stressful—a single kick may decide the outcome of a whole match or competition. The expectations involved can weigh on the taker's mind. If properly managed, it will make him extra alert and careful as he kicks the ball. If the stress becomes too excessive for him, though, he may lose composure and stumble as he goes to kick the ball.

In the same way, when stress is too much for you, the consequences are dire. You stay in a default state of depression or anxiety, which affects your mental health, making it difficult to cope with work, relationships, and regular daily activities. The heart is overworked, your blood pressure is high, and stress-induced chemicals released by the brain permeate the bloodstream. In excess, the chemicals affect cell regeneration. The entire state combines to deplete the immune system, making the individual more susceptible to various minor and terminal diseases, including heart attack and cancer.

Despite this, it is important to understand that stress is a stimulus, and it is how the body reacts to it that determines its impact. For example, even good stress, like going out on a date with someone you fancy, can generate negative outcomes. Usually, everyone tries to appear clever, smart, and likable on a first date. That is why your heart beats faster as you choose the best answer to a question from your date. However, if you fail to manage the stress carefully, you may lose confidence. Then, you may start to worry that your date may not like you or, worse, that he/she won't show up. As you can see, the situations can be similar, while the responses are dissimilar. So your perception of the stressor is vital.

That is why the lines that differentiate good stress from bad stress are not always clear. Good stress can become bad if it is not managed properly. That also means that bad stress can become good stress. The key factors in determining the impact of stress are its duration, the amount, and your response to the stress.

Therefore, understanding and learning to manage stress is an essential hack for a happy, productive life.

CHAPTER 2

COMMON STRESS TRIGGERS YOU HAVE BEEN IGNORING

"It's not the load that breaks you down, it's the way you carry it."
—*Lou Holtz*

You need to handle stress properly, or it will hand you bad outcomes. It's that simple!

Some years ago, I was working on a big project. The task was bigger than anything I had ever been assigned, and this got me really excited. I worked myself up to a fever pitch so badly that I couldn't seem to actually work. A week into my task and I still had nothing concrete. The whole team was waiting for my output—everyone knew I was the best man for the task, but I had nothing! I couldn't explain my unproductivity. My excitement began to give way to dread and a loss of confidence. Luckily for me, the team leader took me aside, and we had a storming session on how I could start. Of course, at the session, I was simply reminded of things that I already knew. However, that session got me revitalized, and I started on the task and finally completed it.

What was the source of my stress? Why couldn't I act until I was prompted? I was having trouble sleeping at night because I had got burgled a few days before the task was due to start. I woke up feeling grumpy and unrefreshed. That translated into my unproductivity and gloomy moods. This is an example of what stress can do to anybody that gives it a chance.

More importantly, though, this story shows why it is important to stay alert and identify triggers early. My biggest mistake was not knowing that I was triggered by poor sleep. You need to be able to identify the most potent triggers around you and work to defeat them. If you can avoid or defeat the triggers of stress, you are already halfway to avoiding chronic stress.

However, our differences in personality and perception mean that stressors are different for everyone. What stresses you out may be a mere inconvenience for another person, but certain stressors are common for almost everybody. Their mere presence should make you more alert and focused on identifying the first telltale signs of chronic stress. Let us take a look at some of them.

Common stress triggers

1. **Financial issues:** We all worry about paying our loans and the credit card bill at the end of every month. We worry about doing the taxes and getting the deductibles. You may even get in conflict with loved ones about how you spend your money. In fact, according to the American Psychiatric Association (APA), money issues are the biggest stressor around. When we do not make enough to cover our wants and needs, it may precipitate stress.
2. **Work-related issues:** Most people end up at jobs they hate because they have to make a living. Many push themselves to the extreme working multiple

jobs, and some are in the throes of unemployment. All these can be potent stressors. In addition, complex tasks at work, too much responsibility, a toxic work environment, and deadlines can also pile extra pressure on your shoulders.

3. **Personal relationships:** Triggers in your relationships are not limited to the behaviors of toxic people. Stressors may also come from irreconcilable differences and conflict with good people. This can end the relationship, making you lose an important person in your life. Stress can also come from pressures to make commitments or fulfill your responsibilities to other people. For example, you and your partner may not be meeting each other's sexual and emotional needs, and that could lead to some serious stress.

4. **Parenting pressure:** Every parent is afraid of damaging or not doing enough for their kids. You will worry about being there for them while also keeping a job so that you can provide for their material needs. That means you are occupying different roles that you want to excel at. The workload and emotional attachment that come from that can cause you a ton of stress. So you must build a routine that facilitates a healthy balance.

5. **Traumatic events**: My burgled house kept me under stress for weeks after the event. Many other traumatic events can cause the same effect. It is even worse when you are the direct victim of stress. Serious attention has been paid to Post Traumatic Stress Disorder in recent decades because of the effects it causes. If you have gotten an upheaval, you may be under stress without knowing.

How to know when you are stressed

The five stressors I have mentioned here are not the only triggers of stress, but I hope I have given you enough knowledge to spot most of them. Just to be sure, I will also show you how to know when you are being stressed excessively.

When you are stressed, the following symptoms may occur:

- **Psychological symptoms:** You become more worried, anxious, lose concentration or forget things easily.
- **Emotional signs:** You become moody, frustrated, or angry at everything.
- **Physical signs:** You gain or lose weight, have high blood pressure, changed sexual appetite, illness, poor sleep, or fatigue.
- **Behavioral signs:** You may lose interest in the things you used to love, stop taking care of yourself, or develop eating disorders or substance abuse.

If several of these signs pop up simultaneously without any viable explanation, you need to analyze your life pattern to discover the stressor putting you through hell.

CHAPTER 3

THE VICIOUS CYCLE BETWEEN STRESS AND ILLNESS

"Stress-related disease emerges, predominantly, out of the fact that we so often activate a physiological system that has evolved for responding to acute physical emergencies, but we turn it on for months on end, worrying about mortgages, relationships, and promotions."
—Robert Sapolsky

When you are stressed, the body undergoes some changes to perform better at certain functions. The brain prioritizes reaction (fight-or-flight), increasing blood flow to the limbs and reducing its supply to other vital internal organs. These organs are crucial to the process that keeps you alive, but they get neglected temporarily to improve your performance.

The body cannot hold this position for long. It wasn't built to remain in a prolonged state of stress. So the ideal thing is for you to return to a normal state as soon as possible. However, if you do not respond to stress the right way, it can become a long-term part of your life.

Therefore, the body will be under more strain, which increases the risk of severe diseases. If you need further proof, consider the stats below:

- Four out of every five clinic visits worldwide are due to conditions aggravated by chronic stress.
- 43% of the world's total population has at least one health disorder caused by persistent stress.
- Stress-related layoffs and absent days cost the US $300 billion yearly.

Why should you be worried?

Chronic stress impairs the immune system and reduces the body's ability to combat the invaders. It weakens your defense against diseases. Stress itself produces various symptoms like nausea, fatigue, insomnia, elevated heart and pulse rates, shortness of breath, body aches, migraine, and muscular problems. In fact, let me give you a quick walk through some common stress-related disorders.

Common stress-induced illnesses

1. **Psychogenic fever:** Unlike normal fever caused by a virus, this type of fever is caused by emotional turmoil and chronic stress, and the body temperature is not as high as that of fever. More common among young women, stress is a major component of this ailment.
2. **Stomach upset:** By reducing blood flow to the gastrointestinal system, stress can cause digestion issues. This may lead to nausea, abdominal pain, constipation, indigestion, and diarrhea. It can also aggravate existing health conditions like irritable bowel disease, ulcers, and colitis.
3. **Depression:** When stress is prolonged, the brain continues to produce chemicals like dopamine, cortisol, and norepinephrine serotonin. Corticosteroid hormone production may then suffer a gradual decline and cause a chemical imbalance

that facilitates depression.

4. **Asthma and allergies:** Stress triggers the mast cells to release histamine. This is one of the chemicals released when we have an allergic reaction. Therefore, when stress is prolonged, it can worsen diseases such as asthma or other allergies.

5. **Obesity:** There are various ways by which stress contributes to obesity. For example, high-stress levels disrupt the digestive process. It also disrupts sleep, which leads to a potential increase in belly fat. Finally, it may cause an eating disorder by creating cravings for refined carbohydrates. By contributing to obesity, stress is indirectly responsible for diseases like cancer, diabetes, and heart disease.

6. **Heart disease:** When people have a cardiovascular attack, doctors tell them to rest and stay away from stressful activities. This is because stress can cause and aggravate heart diseases. It also reduces the chances of surviving a heart attack.

7. **Diabetes:** Stress increases your blood sugar levels and creates cravings for unhealthy foods that can make you overweight. Getting obese is the primary risk factor for diabetes.

8. **Alzheimer's disease:** Stress, especially from trauma, hastens brain lesions' formation, causing the progressions of the symptoms of Alzheimer's disease. People who have lived with chronic stress often have poor memory-retention skills as they grow older.

9. **Accelerated aging:** In both children and adults, stress can cause people to look older than their age. The body is overworked, damaging the cells but also reducing the ability to regenerate. This slows down healing and accelerates aging.

Stress can lead to illness, and illness can put you under stress. Whatever the case, chronic stress should not be allowed to persist for long. It causes depletion of the body's reserves, causes hormonal and chemical imbalances, and overworks the human body. To stay healthy, fix chronic stress.

CHAPTER 4

10 ESSENTIAL TECHNIQUES FOR RELIEVING STRESS

"How we perceive a situation and how we react to it is the basis of our stress. If you focus on the negative in any situation, you can expect high-stress levels. However, if you try and see the good in the situation, your stress levels will greatly diminish."
—*Catherine Pulsifer*

The bad news is that excessive stress is dangerous and can cause plenty of problems for you. It can render you ill, sad, and unproductive. For most people, stress creeps upon them and continues to build up to toxic levels. It then steals emotional and mental control for them, leaves them feeling helpless and tired.

Luckily, the good news is that you can fix stress. Yes, you cannot avoid stress, but you can build certain habits to minimize its effects. This chapter will give you ten essential techniques that will provide you with an edge over stress.

1. Do diaphragmatic breathing

You might also know it as abdominal and belly breathing. The exercise was originally designed for people with chronic obstructive pulmonary diseases. Diaphragmatic breathing engages the diaphragm, stomach, and abdominal muscles. It relieves stress by lowering cortisol levels and heart rate and increasing endurance for physical exercises. Here is how to go about it:

1. Sit or lie (on the floor or elevated surface) down comfortably
2. Relax your shoulders
3. Place one hand on your stomach and the other on your chest
4. Breathe in for one second through your nose (You may feel the air as it moves from your nostril to your abdomen. You may also feel your stomach expanding. It will protrude outward while your chest remains in the original position.)
5. Purse your lips as if drinking through a straw, then gently apply pressure to your stomach as you exhale for about two seconds
6. Repeat the process a couple of times

2. Practice mindfulness

People practice mindfulness because it helps them gather their mental strength. By doing this, they can lower their stress levels and also control their reactions to the stressors. You can enjoy this too. With the newfound strength, you can call those chaotic, wandering, and repetitive thoughts to order.

The point of mindfulness is to focus all your attention on the moment and practice acceptance. Accept the reality of the feelings stressing you out, then turn your attention towards finding peace. This will help you slow down and change your perception of the situation. You will stop overthinking and, therefore, stop the stressors from causing further damage. You will find many mindfulness exercises on the internet. For now, try this mindful eating exercise:

1. When you go to lunch, avoid talking or engaging in any other task except eating. You can eat in your office or sit separately to avoid being disturbed.

2. Let the food have your undivided attention. Savor the flavor, taste, and chewiness. Engage your senses in tasting, chewing, smelling, and swallowing your meal.

3. Make meditation a regular staple

If you practice it regularly, meditation can turn your life around. I emphasize the term "practice" because many people turn away when the first few attempts are not of much help. If you do it right, meditation doesn't just relieve you of stress. It also makes you more tolerant and, therefore, less likely to be stressed by certain events. Meditation also improves your emotional and physical wellbeing in the long term.

You are going to love using meditation as your go-to method of relieving stress. If you are stressed at work, meditate; on the road, you are good to go; at a seminar, nothing is stopping you from meditating. All you need is to find the meditation techniques that work for you.

I can fill this entire book with meditation techniques, but I won't. Instead, I will recommend one, and you can use the internet to discover more techniques. Try breathing meditation:

1. Take a comfortable position, sitting or standing

2. Then, cast your gaze into the distance with your mouth slightly open
3. Slowly close your eyes
4. Make sure your face is relaxed, then open your eyes slowly
5. Repeat

4. Learn to let go

We all hold onto painful and negative memories. It is an innate need for humanity to wonder what could have been and mourn our losses. However, grief must end at a stage. If you keep holding on, then you cannot move forward. This aggravates your stress levels as baggage from the past will impair your mental health and weigh you down in the present.

There are two crucial factors to regaining your freedom. First, you must realize that it is impossible to control everything. "Life happens," as they say. We all go through ups and downs. You must be ready to accept the bad times when they come around and work your way out of them.

The second factor is forgiveness—for yourself and other people. Nobody has ever fixed a problem by assigning blames. The only thing blaming ever does is escalate conflicts. Accept that it is human to make mistakes, and it is also human to forgive. Then you will realize that you are going to be fine. You will move on. The following tips will help you let go:

- State the lessons you learned from the experience
- Create physical distance by getting rid of things that remind you of the experience
- Find distraction and, ultimately, growth in a new skill or hobby

5. Exercise regularly

Science has proven that physical exercises reduce stress and improve your health. For example, studies show that running can increase your lifespan, reduce cortisol levels, and improve your mood, among other benefits. When you engage in any aerobic activity, blood flow improves, and your body's ability to use oxygen increases to make you stronger. Physical exercises also release feel-good chemicals (endorphins) into the bloodstream. This boosts your mood. In general, exercising is a good way to avoid worrying by shifting attention from your mind to your body.

You don't need to spend several hours each day at the gym. Regular exercising doesn't take much time out of your busy schedule. The American Heart Association (AHA) says you are good with just 150 minutes of moderate workout every week. You can split these between three to four days. Exercises you might like include biking, tennis, squash, dancing, Pilates, yoga, and running.

6. Eat right

The food you eat can either be good or bad for your stress levels and general health. There is no middle ground. So you have to choose wisely. Healthy foods give your nervous and immune systems the nutrients they need to regulate your stress levels; they also don't stress the body further. However, the best approach is to have a generally healthy diet. Here are some tips to get you started:
- Replace caffeine with herbal tea
- Replace soda and processed drinks with fresh fruit juice and warm milk
- Try organic products
- Reduce alcohol consumption
- Eat dark chocolate

- Replace regular flour with whole grains and sweet potato
- Eat more fresh fruits and leafy greens
- Reduce steak and go for fish
- Drink a lot of water daily

7. Boost your time management skills

Do you ever wonder while some people seem to complete their tasks in time while others struggle? Stress itself can be a function of time. You need to learn to efficiently complete your tasks to avoid being weighed down by deadlines.

By controlling how you spend your time, you become more efficient with time and effort. Therefore, you become more productive and complete tasks faster. You get more done. And even better, you have more time to relax and take care of yourself.

Most of our wasted effort is due to distractions and procrastination—these two work hand in hand to steal your time. The day is gone before you know it, and you get stressed about not accomplishing your aim. The key is to get started and stay away from things that distract you.

To do this, you must understand your goals and the best ways to use your time to accomplish them. That requires planning, a motif that will be repeated a few times in this chapter. The key to planning is getting the priorities right. If you can't accomplish every goal, you want to make sure the important ones are done. However, urgency sometimes supersedes importance. In the quest to optimize your time and energy, do the important or urgent things first. It helps if you:

- Start early
- Avoid multitasking
- Give yourself small breaks to relax and recharge

8. Get adequate rest and sleep

When our body needs a break, we get some rest or sleep. However, sometimes stress (or other factors) makes it impossible to sleep. When stress robs you of sleep, it takes away the one time that your body can recharge and repair damaged cells. When you think about it, it happens a lot. I am talking about being too stressed to relax.

This only increases your stress levels and makes the body more vulnerable. It is important to get that sleep, maybe by trying relaxation and meditation techniques to put your mind at ease. Then you can get that good sleep and come back stronger. According to experts, that is around 7-8 hours every night. The following tips can help you relax better:

- Take breaks during work
- Have a sleep routine and get to bed every night at the set time
- Minimize late-night television
- Eat dinner early
- Sleep in a dark, cool room with no noise
- Get comfortable beddings

9. Plan your day ahead

Every year, we make New Year's resolutions and plan towards making them happen, but has it ever crossed your mind that you can also do that every day? I mean, you can plan each day ahead to stay in control. By planning your day, you create a strategy to keep you focused and offer direction. You are prepared, moving with precision from one task to another, to deal with any stressor that might show up.

It is not so difficult. Before going to bed every night, think about the tasks and goals for the following day. Then, create a to-do list, starting with the most important ones. Create a schedule to guide you through the day like a map. Then you can avoid the stress and pressure of being overwhelmed by your tasks. I recommend setting reminders on your phone calendar or getting a planning app from your mobile app store to help you even better.

10. Use the power of routines to your advantage

There is no denying the effect of having a predictable day in which you are certain about everything. Great for your stress levels, but boring. Or so, one would think. You forget that you can't control everything. So you will benefit from a structure that reduces the unpredictability and uncertainty of modern life.

You don't have to stress over what decisions to make or which action to take next. Therefore, it will be easier to maintain a healthy stress level and complete your tasks. That's not so bad, is it? Well, routines also make it easier to dump bad habits and adopt new ones. The almost mechanical process keeps you relaxed, focused, and moving.

CONCLUSION

Thank you for reading this book! I hope you have learned new things about chronic stress and how to deal with it.

Perhaps the most important message you should take from the book is that "Stress isn't necessarily bad all the time, but it is bad when it is negative, excessive and long-term." A bit of stress can help you fight for longer and try harder for the things you want, but stress does not deserve to be your constant companion. Stress can be the defense mechanism, the shield you need against threats. But if you have to lug the shield about for the whole day, it will weigh you down and cause you significant harm.

With that in mind, where do you go from here? What is the next step you have to take?

The next thing to do is to take action to deal with stress. It is not enough for you to know the techniques. You have to be ready to put them into action. Most of them are fairly simple habits, but they all have great impacts. You do not need to start all ten techniques at once, but you should have a clear plan to integrate them all into your daily routine. As Pablo Picasso said, "Action is the foundational element of success." Take action now against stress to regain control of your life, boost productivity levels and stay happy all day long.

Always remember that chronic stress kills, but first, it maims.

Stay safe and happy!

ABOUT THE AUTHOR

Vinh Nguyen sees himself as the "happiest author on earth." His life goal is to help as many people as possible to learn to be happy. One book at a time. He believes that you can be happy if you choose to exercise the power you already have within yourself.

Vinh was born and bred in Vietnam and lives (happily ever after) in New Zealand.

BY THE SAME AUTHOR

- Start Your Exercise Routine and Keep the Motivation Forever: A Simple Guide for Your Life Fitness

- How to Sleep Faster Better Smarter Naturally: An Essential Easy Guide for Your Best Life

- Meditate for Life: A Simple Guide to Start Your Daily Meditation Journey and Love It Forever

Printed in Great Britain
by Amazon